Mathem
with Me

5

CALCULATORS

Lila Bental

Stanley Thornes (Publishers) Ltd

First published in 1986 by:
Stanley Thornes (Publishers) Ltd
Old Station Drive
Leckhampton
CHELTENHAM GL53 0DN
England

British Library Cataloguing in Publication Data

Bental, L.M.
    Mathematics with meaning.
    Unit 5
    Pupils' book
    1. Mathematics—Examinations, questions, etc.
    I. Title
    510'.76   QA43

ISBN 0–85950–531–6

Typeset by Tech-Set, Gateshead, Tyne & Wear,
in 11/14 Avant Garde Book.
Printed and bound in Great Britain at The Bath Press, Avon.

Calculators

In Unit 1 we used the calculator to help us understand place value and the decimal point.

We will find out more about numbers and **operations** ($+ - \times \div$) with the calculator in Part 4.

Most of our calculating in everyday life has to do with money, but we could use the calculator for all the measures in Unit 3.

To make sure we get the right answer (or **result**) we need:
1   to know a few facts;
2   to know our own calculators;
3   to do some thinking about the question and the answer;
4   to press the right **keys** in the right order;
5   to **check** that the answer makes sense.

Part 1   Knowing a Few Facts

Make sure that you know the following by heart:

(A) Facts from Unit 1

   a)   The additions in Exercises 3 and 4 (reprinted on page 29).
   b)   The subtractions in Exercises 5 and 6 (reprinted on page 29).
   c)   The multiplication tables for 2, 5 and 10 (reprinted on page 30).
   d)   The division tables for 2, 5 and 10 (reprinted on page 30).

Get a friend to test you on these.

(B) Facts from Unit 3

   a)   100 pence equal   £1.
   b)   1000 grams equal   1 kilogram.
   c)   1000 metres equal   1 kilometre.
   d)   100 centimetres equal 1 metre.
   e)   10 millimetres equal   1 centimetre.
   f)   60 seconds equal   1 minute.
   g)   60 minutes equal   1 hour.

Try to learn these parrot fashion.

Get a friend to test you.

1

Part 2   Getting to Know your Calculator

EXERCISE 1

a) Switch on to start.

b) Look at the **display**. It should display 0 (zero).

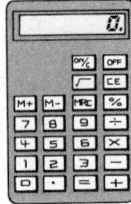

c) **Clear** the **memory**.
The work in this unit does not need the memory.

d) Take care to press the key you want **once** only.
Press these keys: $2 + 4 =$
The result on the display should be 6.

e) Press the 2 three times.
Look at the display.
It shows 2 2 2 (two hundred and twenty two).

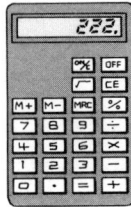

- -

EXERCISE 2

a) Clear the display.

b) Press these keys, watching the display: $4 + 2 + 1 + 3 + 6 =$
The displayed number changes as the calculator adds each number on.
It shows you the **running total** when you press +

c) Watch the display while you key in $5 + 5 + 5 + 5 + 5 =$
The final total will be 25.
We say you took ten **steps** in this calculation.
Each time you key in a number or a sign, it counts as one step.

d) Do calculation **c)** again.
Copy out the diagram below, showing what you see on the display as
you press the keys

Step	Key		Display	
1	5	⟶	5	
2	+	⟶	5	(Total)
3	5	⟶	5	
4	+	⟶	10	(Total)
5	5	⟶	5	
6	+	⟶	15	(Total)
7	5	⟶	5	
8	+	⟶	20	(Total)
9	5	⟶	5	
10	=	⟶	25	(Total)

Your final total is 25

- -

EXERCISE 3

Make up another calculation and draw a step diagram to show what
happens.

Ask your teacher to check your work.

- -

EXERCISE 4

The calculator puts the numbers in columns for you, so this sum
$$\begin{array}{r} 72 \\ 43 \\ + 59 \\ \hline \\ = \end{array}$$

is keyed in as: $72 + 43 + 59 =$

Do these on the calculator and write down the answers:

a)
$$\begin{array}{r} 72 \\ 43 \\ + 59 \\ \hline \\ = \end{array}$$

b)
$$\begin{array}{r} 94 \\ + 5 \\ \hline \\ = \end{array}$$

c)
$$\begin{array}{r} 102 \\ + 64 \\ \hline \\ = \end{array}$$

d)
$$\begin{array}{r} 540 \\ + 3 \\ \hline \\ = \end{array}$$

3

A number with no sign is **positive** (+). So 27 is the same as +27.
Check by doing these:

e) $+5+20 =$ _25_
$5+20 =$ _25_

f) $+12+8 =$ _____
$12+8 =$ _____

- -

EXERCISE 5

$$\begin{array}{r} 47 \\ - \ 26 \\ \hline = \end{array}$$ should be keyed in as $47-26=$

Do these on the calculator and write down the answers:

a)
$$\begin{array}{r} 47 \\ - \ 26 \\ \hline 21 \end{array}$$

b)
$$\begin{array}{r} 125 \\ - \ 109 \\ \hline 016 \end{array}$$

c)
$$\begin{array}{r} 14 \\ - \ 7 \\ \hline 7 \end{array}$$

d)
$$\begin{array}{r} 33 \\ - \ 18 \\ \hline = \end{array}$$

Mark your own work.

You may have found some mistakes.

It is best to <u>do each calculation twice over</u> to make sure that you have pressed the right keys.

- -

EXERCISE 6

$$\begin{array}{r} 25 \\ \times \ 4 \\ \hline = \end{array}$$ should be keyed in as $25 \times 4 =$

Do these on the calculator and write down the results:

a)
$$\begin{array}{r} 25 \\ \times \ 4 \\ \hline 100 \end{array}$$

b)
$$\begin{array}{r} 6 \\ \times \ 5 \\ \hline 30 \end{array}$$

c)
$$\begin{array}{r} 3 \\ \times \ 25 \\ \hline 75 \end{array}$$

d)
$$\begin{array}{r} 50 \\ \times \ 2 \\ \hline 100 \end{array}$$

- -

4

EXERCISE 7

We can read $10\overline{)100}$ as: ten into a hundred
or   a hundred divided by ten.

$10\overline{)100}$ should be keyed in as $100 \div 10 =$ 10

Do these on the calculator and write down the results:

a) $5\overline{)15}$ 3

b) $10\overline{)60}$ 6

c) $2\overline{)500}$

d) $6\overline{)30}$ 5

Get a friend to check your results.

EXERCISE 8

There is a rule in mathematics that tells us to do multiplication and division before addition and subtraction, when they are in the same calculation.

$$2 + 6 - 8 \times 3 \div 2 + 4 =$$
FIRST   X   ÷
THEN   +   −

RESULT = ?

So to get the result of $5 + 3 \times 4$
we do 3×4 first, which is 12
then $5 + 12$ which gives us 17.

Do these in your book:

a) $4 + 6 \times 2 =$ 20 (12)

b) $2 + 3 \times 5 =$ _____

To do $10 - 6 \div 2$
we do $6 \div 2$ first, which is 3
then $10 - 3$ which gives us 7.

Do these:

c) $6 - 4 \div 2 =$ _____

d) $20 - 10 \div 5 =$ _____

5

Some calculators do the operations in the right order for you.

e) Try it, with **a), b), c)** and **d),** pressing the keys in the order in which the numbers and signs are printed.
Write down the displayed answers.
Check the results.
If they are different find out how your calculator works, and do **a), b), c)** and **d)** again, correctly.

There may be other keys on your calculator.
We do not need them yet.

- -

Part 3   Thinking

Give yourself some thinking time before doing a calculation.
Think about the question and the keys you will need to press.

Think about <u>what kind of result</u> you expect.
Then you can tell if your result is roughly correct.

EXERCISE 1

Which of these will have a result with a <u>5</u> in the <u>units</u> place?

If the result has a 5 in the units place, put a $\sqrt{}$; if not, put a ✕.

a)	$10 + 5$	**e)**	$15 - 5$	**i)**	5×3	**m)**	$50 \div 10$
b)	$20 - 5$	**f)**	$12 + 5$	**j)**	10×3	**n)**	$35 \div 7$
c)	$10 - 3$	**g)**	$25 + 5$	**k)**	$36 + 15$	**o)**	$45 \div 5$
d)	$100 + 2$	**h)**	$42 + 3$	**l)**	$12 \div 2$	**p)**	18×5

Mark your work.

- -

EXERCISE 2

Try to spot which of these will have a result <u>ending in zero</u> (0 in the units place).

If it has, put a $\checkmark$; if not, put a $\times$.

a) $7 - 7 = $ 〇   **e)** $100 \div 10 = 10$ **i)** $14 \div 2$ **m)** $72 - 3$

b) $95 \times 0 = 0$ **f)** $10 \times 10 = 100$ **j)** $38 - 8 = 30$ **n)** $255 - 15 = 240$

c) $3 \times 10 = 30$ **g)** $8 \div 4$ **k)** $42 + 8 = 50$ **o)** $25 \div 5$

d) $40 \div 4 = 10$ **h)** 6×2 **l)** $51 + 6$ **p)** $20 \div 2 = 10$

Mark your work.

HOOP-LA

RING AN EVEN NUMBER
WIN A PRIZE

EXERCISE 3

Try to guess which of these will have a result which is an <u>even number</u>.

If it is even, put a $\checkmark$; if it is odd, put a $\times$.

a) 4×2 **c)** $3 + 3$ **e)** 2×7 **g)** $10 + 9$

b) $2 + 4$ **d)** 9×2 **f)** 3×5 **h)** $8 + 15$

(Reminder: You need only look at the units. 0, 2, 4, 6 and 8 are even.)

Ask your teacher to check your work.

7

EXERCISE 4

Guess (estimate) whether these will have results with figures in the tens place.

If there is a <u>ten</u> in the result, put a $\sqrt{}$; if not, put a ✕.

a)	$6 + 10$	**e)**	$5 + 1$	**i)**	1×8	**m)**	10×7
b)	2×10	**f)**	$28 - 6$	**j)**	$19 + 22$	**n)**	$80 \div 10$
c)	$10 - 3$	**g)**	$20 - 18$	**k)**	8×2	**o)**	$30 \div 10$
d)	$9 + 41$	**h)**	$12 - 4$	**l)**	5×9	**p)**	$60 \div 6$

Mark your work.

If you have made any mistakes ask your teacher for help.

- -

EXERCISE 5

Estimate whether the result will contain any hundreds, for each of these.

If there is a <u>hundred</u> in the result, put a $\sqrt{}$; if not, put a ✕.

a)	$219 + 21$	**d)**	$600 - 200$	**g)**	742×0
b)	$146 - 100$	**e)**	$378 + 291$	**h)**	$956 - 0$
c)	20×10	**f)**	$24 + 62$	**i)**	$99 + 10$

Get a friend to check these.

- -

EXERCISE 6

Look at the first number (in the box) in each of these.
Estimate whether the result will be bigger than the first number.
The sign gives you the clue.

Put a $\sqrt{}$ if the result is bigger than the first number; if not, put a ✕.

a)	$\boxed{5} \times 2$	**d)**	$\boxed{10} - 1$	**g)**	$\boxed{10} \div 5$	**j)**	$\boxed{50} - 25$
b)	$\boxed{10} + 2$	**e)**	$\boxed{6} \div 2$	**h)**	$\boxed{100} + 100$	**k)**	$\boxed{14} \div 2$
c)	$\boxed{9} \times 10$	**f)**	$\boxed{25} - 5$	**i)**	$\boxed{100} \div 2$	**l)**	$\boxed{8} \times 5$

m) Which signs gave a result bigger than the first number?

Mark your own work.

If you have made any mistakes ask your teacher for help.

- -

EXERCISE 7

Look at the first number (in the box) in each of these.
Will the result be more than, less than, or the same as the first number?

Write M for more, L for less, S for same.

a) $\boxed{10} + 4 - 4$ d) $\boxed{25} + 6 + 2$ g) $\boxed{12} - 12 + 3$

b) $\boxed{16} + 3 - 1$ e) $\boxed{15} + 9 - 9$ h) $\boxed{7} - 7 + 5$

c) $\boxed{5} - 3 + 4$ f) $\boxed{11} - 1 + 10$ i) $\boxed{100} + 75 - 75$

Mark your work.

Ask your teacher to look over your work.

- -

EXERCISE 8

Do you expect the results of these to be **positive** or **negative?**

Write + for positive, − for negative.

a) $6 + 3 + 9 + 27$ e) $-10 - 5 + 12$ i) $20 \div 10$

b) $8 - 17 - 4$ f) $11 - 6 + 3$ j) 10×8

c) $-3 + 15$ g) 4×5 k) $10 \div 2$

d) $20 - 10 - 5 - 2$ h) $8 \div 4$ l) 7×2

Ask your teacher to mark these.

- -

EXERCISE 9

See if you can estimate whether these results will be <u>whole numbers</u>, fractions, or **mixed numbers**.

Write W for <u>whole number</u>, F for fractions, and M for <u>mixed numbers</u>.

a)	$10 \div 2$	**c)**	4×5	**e)**	$1 \div 4$	**g)**	$1 \div 5$
b)	$1 \div 2$	**d)**	$20 \div 5$	**f)**	$5 \div 2$	**h)**	$7 \div 2$

Mark these yourself.

If you have made any errors, ask your teacher for help.

- -

Part 4   Using the Calculator

(A) Numbers and Operations

EXERCISE 1

We make fewer mistakes if we press fewer keys.
So if you have to <u>add</u> the same number <u>many times</u>, use <u>multiply</u> and cut down the number of steps.

Copy these out, do the calculation <u>in 4 steps</u> and fill in the spaces:

a) $5 + 5 + 5 + 5 = 5 \times 4 = 20$
b) $6 + 6 + 6 + 6 = 6 \times \underline{\hspace{1cm}} = \underline{\hspace{2cm}}$
c) $7 + 7 + 7 + 7 + 7 = 7 \times \underline{\hspace{1cm}} = \underline{\hspace{2cm}}$
d) $2 + 2 + 2 + 2 + 2 + 2 + 2 = 2 \times \underline{\hspace{1cm}} = \underline{\hspace{2cm}}$
e) $25 + 25 + 25 + 25 + 25 + 25 = 25 \times \underline{\hspace{1cm}} = \underline{\hspace{2cm}}$
f) $15 + 15 + 15 = 15 \times \underline{\hspace{1cm}} = \underline{\hspace{2cm}}$

Mark these yourself.

- -

EXERCISE 2

Press $7 + 3 =$ Look at the result.
Press $3 + 7 =$ Look at the result.

You should see 10 as the result in both cases.

Write out these pairs of additions with the results:

a) $\begin{cases} 10 + 5 = \rule{2cm}{0.4pt} \\ 5 + 10 = \rule{2cm}{0.4pt} \end{cases}$

b) $\begin{cases} 8 + 12 = \rule{2cm}{0.4pt} \\ 12 + 8 = \rule{2cm}{0.4pt} \end{cases}$

c) $\begin{cases} 18 + 2 = \rule{2cm}{0.4pt} \\ 2 + 18 = \rule{2cm}{0.4pt} \end{cases}$

d) $\begin{cases} 6 + 14 = \rule{2cm}{0.4pt} \\ 14 + 6 = \rule{2cm}{0.4pt} \end{cases}$

e) $\begin{cases} 125 + 75 = \rule{2cm}{0.4pt} \\ 75 + 125 = \rule{2cm}{0.4pt} \end{cases}$

f) $\begin{cases} 55 + 45 = \rule{2cm}{0.4pt} \\ 45 + 55 = \rule{2cm}{0.4pt} \end{cases}$

g) $\begin{cases} 99 + 1 = \rule{2cm}{0.4pt} \\ 1 + 99 = \rule{2cm}{0.4pt} \end{cases}$

h) $\begin{cases} 89 + 11 = \rule{2cm}{0.4pt} \\ 11 + 89 = \rule{2cm}{0.4pt} \end{cases}$

- -

EXERCISE 3

a) Press $-26 + 47 =$ Look at the result.
Does it give the same result as $47 - 26 =$?

b) Calculate $\quad 18 - 5 = \rule{2.5cm}{0.4pt}$,
and $\qquad\qquad -5 + 18 = \rule{2.5cm}{0.4pt}$
Write down the results.

c) Make up three more subtractions.
Do them two ways and write them out, as in **b)**.

Ask your teacher to mark your work.

- -

EXERCISE 4

If you are finding the difference between two numbers, you subtract the smaller one from the larger one.
So the difference between 75 and 100 is found by pressing $100 - 75 =$ which gives 25.

Key in the larger number first.

If you press $75 - 100 =$ you will get -25. The right answer is a positive number, not a negative one.

Write out and complete these sentences:

a) The difference between   2 and   7 is _____ .
b) The difference between 45 and 100 is _____ .
c) The difference between 250 and 150 is _____ .
d) The difference between 25 and 100 is _____ .
e) The difference between 20 and 15 is _____ .

Make up and write out two more differences.

- -

EXERCISE 5

Copy out this table and complete a), b), c) and d).
Use the calculator to find the results.

	Operation	Result	Operation	Result
a)	5×3	_____	3×5	_____
b)	2×7	_____	7×2	_____
c)	6×5	_____	5×6	_____
d)	10×4	_____	4×10	_____
e)	_____	_____	_____	_____
f)	_____	_____	_____	_____
g)	_____	_____	_____	_____

You probably expected the two results in each example to be the same.

Make up three more pairs of multiplications, e), f) and g).
Put them into the table.

- -

EXERCISE 6

	Operation	Result	Operation	Result
1)	10 ÷ 5	_____	5 ÷ 10	_____
2)	20 ÷ 2	_____	2 ÷ 20	_____
3)	8 ÷ 4	_____	4 ÷ 8	_____
4)	_____	_____	_____	_____
5)	_____	_____	_____	_____
6)	_____	_____	_____	_____

a) Copy out this table.

b) Use the calculator to find the results and fill them in.
The two results in each example are <u>not the same</u>.
For   10 ÷ 5   we can say, 'How many fives are in ten?'
This is <u>not the same</u> as, 'How many tens are in five?'
(If you are not sure, get some small objects and divide them into sets.
Talk to your teacher about it.)
We must do division in the right order.

c) Make up three more pairs of divisions and put them into the table as
4), **5)** and **6)**.

Show your work to your teacher.

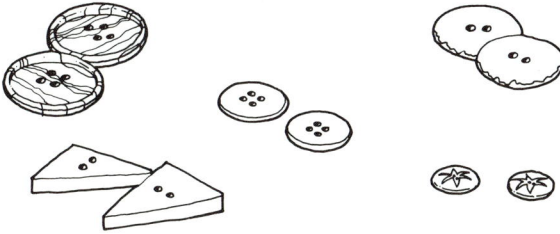

- -

EXERCISE 7

When we use the calculator to <u>check</u> our divisions, we sometimes multiply.

a) Do this in your head: 45 ÷ 9

b) Check your answer on the calculator.
You could either   press 45 ÷ 9 =
            or   you could check your answer by multiplying it by
                    9 and looking for 45 on the display

13

c) Do this in your head. Write down your answer.
Check with the calculator and write down the keys you press.
$35 \div 5 =$ _____
Keys pressed to check: _____

d) Do these as in **c)**.
   (i) $100 \div 10 =$ _____   (ii) $14 \div 2 =$ _____
       Keys pressed: _____   Keys pressed: _____

e) Do two of your own divisions in your head and check them on the
calculator.
Write them out as in **c)**

Ask your teacher to mark your work.

- -

EXERCISE 8

Odd Numbers

Odd numbers have 1, 3, 5, 7 or 9 in the units place.
For this exercise watch out for the decimal point.

Divide these odd numbers by 2 and write down the results:

a)	5	**b)**	15	**c)**	25	**d)**	35	**e)**	45	**f)**	55
g)	3	**h)**	13	**i)**	23	**j)**	33	**k)**	43	**l)**	53
m)	7	**n)**	17	**o)**	27	**p)**	37	**q)**	47	**r)**	57
s)	9	**t)**	19	**u)**	29	**v)**	39	**w)**	49	**x)**	59
y)	1	**z)**	11								

- -

EXERCISE 9

Dina did one using 15.
She wrote some of her **findings** in this table.
Findings are things you find out.

Number: 15	An Investigation	
Operation	Result	Findings
-1	14	$15 = 1 + 14$
-2	13	$15 = 2 + 13$
$\div 5$	3	$15 = 5 \times 3$
$\times 2$	30	$15 = \frac{1}{2}$ of 30

Find out more about 15.
Write out the table with Dina's findings and add yours to it.

Do an investigation of another number and make a table of your findings.

You could do this with a friend.

Show your teacher your work.

(B) Measures

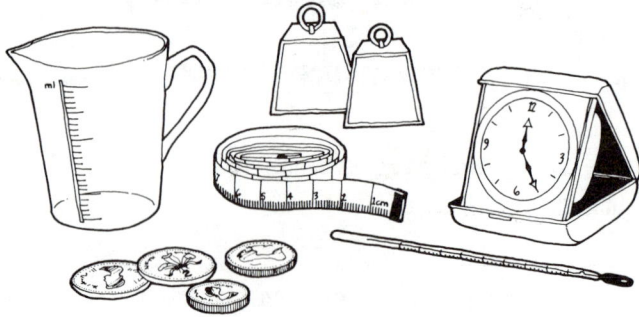

The calculator does not show us the measure.
We must know which measure we are using.
Remember to check that your answer makes sense.

EXERCISE 10

These are all in pounds (£).

Do them and write the answers—don't forget the £ sign.

a) £20 + £14 = __ _____   d) £101 + £92 = __ _____
b) £56 − £24 = __ _____   e) £208 − £58 = __ _____
c) £122 + £19 = __ _____   f) £33 + £77 = __ _____

These are all in pence.

Do them and write the answers—remember the p.

g) 18 p + 18 p = _____   j) 50 p − 16 p = _____
h) 70 p + 24 p = _____   k) 40 p − 7 p = _____
i) 82 p − 12 p = _____   l) 32 p + 46 p = _____

These are mixed.
Choose either pounds or pence to work in.

Write out the answers with either £ or p.

m) £4.25 − 25 p = _____   p) 55 p + £2.40 = _____
n) £6.50 + 40 p = _____   q) £7.94 − 64 p = _____
o) 12 p + £1.04 = _____   r) £5 − 60 p = _____

Mark these yourself.

- -

EXERCISE 11

Calculate these as they are printed here.
Copy them and fill in the result with the £ sign.
Remember the decimal point.

a)   £2.50 + £3.50 = __ _____   c)   £14.50 − £7.50 = __ _____
b)   £15.25 + £1.75 = __ _____   d)   £12.75 − £2.25 = __ _____

Mark your own work.

Ask your teacher to check your marking.

- -

EXERCISE 12

Pence are shown as a decimal fraction of a pound.

$$\frac{1}{2} \text{ (half) of £1} = 50\,p = £0.50$$

a)   Check this by pressing   1 ÷ 2 =
     The display shows 0.5.
     This is the same as 0.50.

We write 50 p for £0.50 but with larger amounts we use the £ sign.

Find these and write them down, using the £ sign.

b)   Half $\left(\frac{1}{2}\right)$ of £3   e)   Half of £9   h)   Half of £15   k)   Half of £21
c)   Half of £5   f)   Half of £11   i)   Half of £17   l)   Half of £31
d)   Half of £7   g)   Half $\left(\frac{1}{2}\right)$ of £13 j)   Half of £19   m)   Half of £41

Mark your own work.

- -

EXERCISE 13

Multiplying Money

The calculator does not show the measure. Your answer must be in £ or p.

To find the cost of 5 comics when 1 comic costs 20 p we multiply (×) the
20 p by 5.

a) Press:

$$20 \times 5 =$$

The answer on the display will be 100.
This means 100 pence which equals £1.

Write in your book: $20\,p \times 5 = 100\,p = £1$.
1 comic costs $20\,p$.
5 comics cost £1.

Use the calculator to do these.
Copy them and put in the result in two forms, using £ and using p.

b) $30\,p \times 5 =$ _____ = _____

c) $25\,p \times 5 =$ _____ = _____

d) $15\,p \times 6 =$ _____ = _____

e) $£2.50 \times 4 =$ _____ = _____

f) $£3.50 \times 5 =$ _____ = _____

g) $80\,p \times 10 =$ _____ = _____

Your calculator may display 17.5 for **f)**. 17.5 is the same as 17.50.

Ask your teacher to mark your work.

— —

EXERCISE 14

Dividing Money

A money answer must be written with £ or p.

a) If 3 children share a £15 prize equally we find out each child's share by dividing (÷).

Press: $15 \div 3 =$
The calculator displays 5.

Write: $£15 \div 3 = £5$.
3 get £15.
1 gets £5.

Use the calculator to work out these divisions.
Copy them out and fill in the answers:

b) $£25 \div 5 =$ _____

c) $£100 \div 2 =$ _____

d) $£15 \div 5 =$ _____

e) $90\,p \div 2 =$ _____

f) $60\,p \div 10 =$ _____

g) $45\,p \div 9 =$ _____

h) $£6 \div 10 =$ _____

i) $£3.50 \div 10 =$ _____

j) $£2.50 \div 5 =$ _____

Mark these yourself.

— —

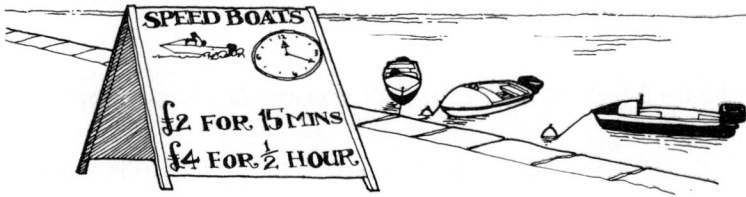

EXERCISE 15

Adding Time

We must name the measure ourselves.
Write full answers.

A. Do these additions of <u>minutes</u>.

a) 20 min + 10 min + 15 min = _____ min
b) 35 min + 5 min + 3 min + 8 min = _____ min

More than 59 minutes would give us <u>hours</u>, so

c) 30 min + 35 min = _____ min = _____ h _____ min
d) 15 min + 15 min + 45 min = _____ min = _____ h _____ min

B. Do these additions of <u>hours</u>.

a) 15 h + 2 h + 5 h + 1 h = _____ h
b) 3 h + 4 h + 12 h = _____ h

More than 23 hours would give us <u>days</u>.

C. Do these additions of <u>days</u>.

a) 2 days + 4 days = _____ days
b) 1 day + 3 days = _____ days

More than 6 days would give us <u>weeks</u>.

D. Do these additions of <u>years</u>.

a) 7 years + 3 years + 2 years = _____ years
b) 20 years + 5 years + 1 year = _____ years

Mark these yourself.

If you have made any mistakes get help from your teacher.

- -

19

EXERCISE 16

We <u>subtract</u> to find out how long it is from one time to another.

Copy these out, do the calculations, then fill in the results and the answers:

a) From 1980 to 1992 is <u>12 years.</u>
Press: 1992 − 1980 =   Result: <u>12</u>

b) From 1972 to 1988 is _____ years.
Press: _____   Result: _____

c) From 1492 to 1992 is _____ _____
Press: _____   Result: _____

d) From 1066 to 1961 is _____ _____
Press: _____   Result: _____

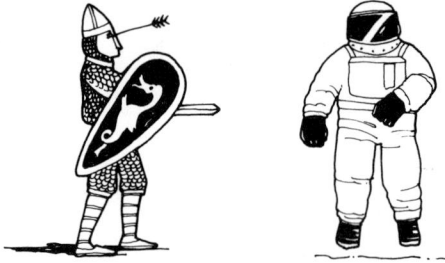

Make up two more examples **e)** and **f)**.
Write them out as above.

Ask your teacher to mark your work.

- -

EXERCISE 17

We can multiply lengths of time.
We must say which measure we mean.

Copy out **a).**
Then work out and write in full **b), c)** and **d).**

a) It takes 10 minutes to read 1 page.
How long does it take to read 6 pages?
We press 10 × 6 =   Result: 60
Answer: 60 minutes or 1 hour.

b) It takes 15 minutes to walk 1 km.
How long does it take to walk 5 km?
Press: _____   Result: _____
Answer: _____

c) It takes 3 minutes to deliver 1 newspaper.
How long does it take to deliver 25 newspapers?
Press: _____   Result: _____
Answer: _____

d) It takes 20 minutes to clean 1 car.
How long does it take to clean 6 cars?
Press: _____   Result: _____
Answer: _____

Mark your own work.

- -

EXERCISE 18

To turn minutes into hours we divide by 60.

So   120 minutes (min) = (120 ÷ 60) hours (h)
                                = 2 hours (h)

Copy and complete:

a)   180 min = _____ h   **c)**   720 min = _____ h
b)   360 min = _____ h   **d)**   300 min = _____ h

The calculator gives us decimal fractions of an hour (<u>not</u> hours and
minutes in the same result).

Try these. Copy out the result shown after pressing ÷ 60 =

e)   90 min = _____ h   **f)**   150 min = _____ h

0.5 of an hour is $\frac{1}{2}$ an hour.

0.5 of an hour is 30 minutes.

Mark your own work.

Ask your teacher to check your marking.

- -

EXERCISE 19

Length

a) What is the total if we add 40 km, 36 km, 150 km and 19 km?
Press: $40 + 36 + 150 + 19 =$
Write down the answer—remember to put km.

b) Make up another addition in kilometres.
Write down what you press and your full answer.

c) What is the difference between 50 km and 27 km?
We subtract to find the difference.
Press: $50 - 27 =$
Write down the answer—remember to put km.

Use the calculator to do these subtractions.

Write down the keys you press and a full answer.

d) 200 km − 30 km   **f)** 30 km − 15 km
e) 100 km − 25 km   **g)** 97 km − 12 km

Mark these yourself.

Show your work to your teacher.

- -

EXERCISE 20

Multiplying Lengths and Distances

We must write down the measure.
Kilometres (km), metres (m), centimetres (cm) and millimetres (mm) are
the common ones.

Write these out, use the calculator to find the results and fill in your answers:

a) 3 cm × 3 = _____ cm   **e)** 10 cm × 5 = _____ _____
b) 7 m × 4 = _____ m   **f)** 8 m × 10 = _____ _____
c) 9 km × 5 = _____ km   **g)** 6 km × 2 = _____ _____
d) 4 mm × 10 = _____ mm   **h)** 9 mm × 2 = _____ _____

When you have the answer, you can give it in another measuring unit,
if you wish.
In   **d)** 40 mm = 4 cm
and in **e)** 50 cm $= \frac{1}{2}$ m.

22

Do these, giving both answers.
i)   3 mm × 10 = _____ mm = _____ cm
j)   20 cm × 5 = _____ cm = _____ m
k)   100 m   × 10 = _____ m   = _____ km

Mark these yourself.

EXERCISE 21

Dividing Lengths and Distances

Do these and write them out with the answers.

a)   25 km ÷ 5 = _____ km   **c)**   16 mm ÷ 2 = _____ mm
b)   80 cm ÷ 2 = _____ cm   **d)**   95 m   ÷ 5 = _____ m

Make up some more divisions.
You may get results with decimal fractions.

Copy out the first two decimal place figures in your answer and write the measuring unit.

We look at <u>rounding</u> in Exercise 28.

Ask your teacher to check your work.

EXERCISE 22

Square Measure for Area

Work on area is also in Unit 2.

The measure must be the same for both lengths.

a) 5 m by 4 m is keyed in as $5 \times 4 =$
The answer is $20\,\text{m}^2$ (square metres).
Write out: The space 5 m by 4 m has an area of 20^2.

Find the areas of these spaces and write them out as in **a)**.

b)	7 m × 2 m	**d)**	5 km × 100 km	**f)**	2 mm × 8 mm
c)	20 cm × 3 cm	**e)**	100 m × 8 m	**g)**	25 km × 4 km

If you are not sure about area, draw **c)** on squared paper.

Use the calculator to work out five large areas of your own.
Write them out. Put the length measures and the square measure in your answer.

Show your work to your teacher.

- -

EXERCISE 23

Cubic Measure for Volume

Work on volume is also in Unit 2, and in Unit 3 Part 5.

We need three lengths with the same measure.
The volume is given in <u>cubic measure</u>.

Work out the volumes of these cuboids.
The first is done for you.

a) $9\,cm \times 2\,cm \times 5\,cm = \underline{90\,cm^3}$ (90 cubic centimetres)
b) $4\,m \times 3\,m \times 2\,m = \underline{\hspace{1cm}}\,m^3$
c) $20\,cm \times 4\,cm \times 2\,cm = \underline{\hspace{1cm}}\,\underline{\hspace{0.5cm}}$
d) $8\,m \times 5\,m \times 3\,m = \underline{\hspace{1cm}}\,\underline{\hspace{0.5cm}}$
e) $10\,mm \times 7\,mm \times 2\,mm = \underline{\hspace{1cm}}\,\underline{\hspace{0.5cm}}$
f) $100\,m \times 50\,m \times 4\,m = \underline{\hspace{1cm}}\,\underline{\hspace{0.5cm}}$
g) Get a shoe box (or another box) and work out its approximate volume.

You may need help with **g)**. (See Unit 2, Exercises 14 to 16.)

You may have to <u>round off</u> the lengths. (See Exercise 28).

Mark a) to f) yourself.

- -

EXERCISE 24

Calculating Litres, Centilitres and Millilitres

We know from Unit 3 that 1 litre (l) has a volume of $1000\,cm^3$.
1 litre = 100 **centilitres** (cl)
1 litre = 1000 millilitres (ml)

A. Use the calculator to do these.
Write them out in full, giving the measure.

a) $5\,\ell + 7\,\ell = \underline{\hspace{1cm}}\,\ell$ **h)** $25\,\ell + 25\,\ell = \underline{\hspace{1cm}}\,\underline{\hspace{0.5cm}}$
b) $25\,\ell - 15\,\ell = \underline{\hspace{1cm}}\,\ell$ **i)** $95\,\ell - 20\,\ell = \underline{\hspace{1cm}}\,\underline{\hspace{0.5cm}}$
c) $8\,\ell \times 4 = \underline{\hspace{1cm}}\,\ell$ **j)** $15\,\ell \times 3 = \underline{\hspace{1cm}}\,\underline{\hspace{0.5cm}}$
d) $5\,m\ell + 2\,m\ell = \underline{\hspace{1cm}}\,m\ell$ **k)** $7\,m\ell + 8\,m\ell = \underline{\hspace{1cm}}\,\underline{\hspace{0.5cm}}$
e) $4\,m\ell \times 2 = \underline{\hspace{1cm}}\,m\ell$ **l)** $20\,m\ell \times 4 = \underline{\hspace{1cm}}\,\underline{\hspace{0.5cm}}$
f) $50\,c\ell + 46\,c\ell = \underline{\hspace{1cm}}\,c\ell$ **m)** $27\,c\ell + 73\,c\ell = \underline{\hspace{1cm}}\,\underline{\hspace{0.5cm}}$
g) $10\,\ell \div 5 = \underline{\hspace{1cm}}\,\ell$ **n)** $30\,\ell \div 6 = \underline{\hspace{1cm}}\,\underline{\hspace{0.5cm}}$

B. Do this with a friend.
Get some numbers from drinks containers and use those to make up some calculations, as in A.

Ask your teacher to mark your work.

- -

EXERCISE 25

Weights

Work on kilograms (kg), grams (g) and milligrams (mg) is also in Unit 3.

With the calculator we can add, subtract, multiply and divide all the weights.
But we must name them. The calculator shows only the numbers.

Work through these and write them out as in **a)**.

a)   12 kg + 64 kg = 76 kg
     Press: 12 + 64 =   Result: 76

b)	42 kg + 19 kg	**e)**	50 mg × 4	**h)**	30 kg ÷ 6
c)	70 g + 150 g	**f)**	163 mg − 72 mg	**i)**	35 g × 2
d)	82 g − 68 g	**g)**	75 g ÷ 5	**j)**	100 kg ÷ 2

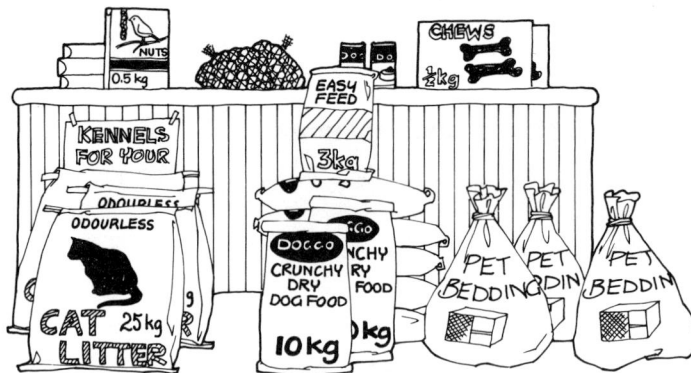

Make up three more weight calculations, **k), l)** and **m)**.
Write them out as in **a)**.

Mark a) to j) yourself.

Ask your teacher to mark k), l) and m).

- -

EXERCISE 26

Since   1000 mg = 1 g
  and   1000 g = 1 kg
we may change the measure we are using.

Copy **a)**, then copy and fill in **b)** and **c)**.

a) $500\,g \times 4 = \underline{2000\,g}$
Press: $500 \times 4 =$ Result: $\underline{2000}$
Our answer is $\underline{2000\,g}$ or $\underline{2\,kg}$

b) $500\,g \times 6 = \underline{\hphantom{XXX}}$
Press: $\underline{\hphantom{XXX}}$ Result: $\underline{\hphantom{XXX}}$
Answer: $\underline{\hphantom{XXX}}$ or $\underline{\hphantom{XXX}}$

c) $400\,mg \times 5 = \underline{\hphantom{XXX}}$
Press: $\underline{\hphantom{XXX}}$ Result: $\underline{\hphantom{XXX}}$
Answer: $\underline{\hphantom{XXX}}$ or $\underline{\hphantom{XXX}}$

Mark these yourself.

EXERCISE 27

Temperature

We can use the calculator to work out temperature changes.
A temperature with no sign in front is above zero.

<u>Step 1</u> Key in the beginning temperature.
<u>Step 2</u> Key in the sign for the change.
<u>Step 3</u> Key in the number of degrees of change.
<u>Step 4</u> Key in =

and the result will be the new temperature.

We must write the measure (° C or ° F).

Copy this table and extend it down your page another five lines.

	Beginning temperature	Change	New temperature
a)	10 °C	−2 °C	8 °C
b)	−5 °C	−4 °C	_____
c)	22 °C	+7 °C	_____
d)	−3 °C	+5 °C	_____
e)	20 °C	−29 °C	_____

Complete **b)**, **c)**, **d)** and **e)**.

Make up, calculate and write in five more examples.

Ask your teacher to mark your work.

(C) Rounding

The calculator result may go to many decimal places.
So we approximate and use rounding.

A Rounding Down
To find how many sixes are in fifty, we press:

$$50 \div 6 = \text{ and the result is } 8.333\ 333\ 3$$

$$\boxed{8.333\ 333\ 3}$$

We want an answer to one decimal place in this exercise, so we look at the second place after the decimal point.
If the figure is less than 5 we round down, that is, we ignore it.
So we ignore the second 3 and use 8.3 as our approximate answer.

Do these and round down your answer. Write them out as in **a)**.

a) $50 \div 6 = 8.333\ 333\ 3 = 8.3$ **d)** $54 \div 7 = $ _____ _____
b) $26 \div 6 = $ _____ _____   **e)** $67 \div 3 = $ _____ _____
c) $43 \div 3 = $ _____ _____   **f)** $15 \div 7 = $ _____ _____

B Rounding Up
To find how many sixes are in forty, we press:

$$40 \div 6 = \text{ and the result is } 6.666\ 666\ 7$$

$$\boxed{6.666\ 666\ 7}$$

This calculator has rounded up the last figure. (Yours may not.)
We look at the figure in the second place of decimals.
If it is 5 or larger, we round up, so we have 6.7 as our approximate answer.

Do these and round up your answer. Write them out as in **a)**.

a) $40 \div 6 = 6.666\ 666\ 7 = 6.7$ **d)** $41 \div 9 = $ _____ _____
b) $19 \div 8 = $ _____ _____   **e)** $20 \div 7 = $ _____ _____
c) $23 \div 4 = $ _____ _____   **f)** $13 \div 4 = $ _____ _____

Ask your teacher to mark your work.

- -

The following addition, subtraction, multiplication and division tables are taken from Unit 1.

0 + 0 = 0	0 + 10 = 10	20 − 0 = 20
1 + 1 = 2	1 + 9 = 10	20 − 1 = 19
2 + 2 = 4	2 + 8 = 10	20 − 2 = 18
3 + 3 = 6	3 + 7 = 10	20 − 3 = 17
4 + 4 = 8	4 + 6 = 10	20 − 4 = 16
5 + 5 = 10	5 + 5 = 10	20 − 5 = 15
6 + 6 = 12	6 + 4 = 10	20 − 6 = 14
7 + 7 = 14	7 + 3 = 10	20 − 7 = 13
8 + 8 = 16	8 + 2 = 10	20 − 8 = 12
9 + 9 = 18	9 + 1 = 10	20 − 9 = 11
10 + 10 = 20	10 + 0 = 10	20 − 10 = 10

10 + 10 = 20	10 + 10 = 20	20 − 11 = 9
11 + 9 = 20	9 + 11 = 20	20 − 12 = 8
12 + 8 = 20	8 + 12 = 20	20 − 13 = 7
13 + 7 = 20	7 + 13 = 20	20 − 14 = 6
14 + 6 = 20	6 + 14 = 20	20 − 15 = 5
15 + 5 = 20	5 + 15 = 20	20 − 16 = 4
16 + 4 = 20	4 + 16 = 20	20 − 17 = 3
17 + 3 = 20	3 + 17 = 20	20 − 18 = 2
18 + 2 = 20	2 + 18 = 20	20 − 19 = 1
19 + 1 = 20	1 + 19 = 20	20 − 20 = 0
20 + 0 = 20	0 + 20 = 20	

10 − 0 = 10	9 − 0 = 9
10 − 1 = 9	8 − 0 = 8
10 − 2 = 8	7 − 0 = 7
10 − 3 = 7	6 − 0 = 6
10 − 4 = 6	5 − 0 = 5
10 − 5 = 5	4 − 0 = 4
10 − 6 = 4	3 − 0 = 3
10 − 7 = 3	2 − 0 = 2
10 − 8 = 2	1 − 0 = 1
10 − 9 = 1	0 − 0 = 0
10 − 10 = 0	

	×2	÷2
0 × 2 = 0	2 × 0 = 0	20 ÷ 2 = 10
1 × 2 = 2	2 × 1 = 2	18 ÷ 2 = 9
2 × 2 = 4	2 × 2 = 4	16 ÷ 2 = 8
3 × 2 = 6	2 × 3 = 6	14 ÷ 2 = 7
4 × 2 = 8	2 × 4 = 8	12 ÷ 2 = 6
5 × 2 = 10	2 × 5 = 10	10 ÷ 2 = 5
6 × 2 = 12	2 × 6 = 12	8 ÷ 2 = 4
7 × 2 = 14	2 × 7 = 14	6 ÷ 2 = 3
8 × 2 = 16	2 × 8 = 16	4 ÷ 2 = 2
9 × 2 = 18	2 × 9 = 18	2 ÷ 2 = 1
10 × 2 = 20	2 × 10 = 20	0 ÷ 2 = 0

	×5	÷5
0 × 5 = 0	5 × 0 = 0	50 ÷ 5 = 10
1 × 5 = 5	5 × 1 = 5	45 ÷ 5 = 9
2 × 5 = 10	5 × 2 = 10	40 ÷ 5 = 8
3 × 5 = 15	5 × 3 = 15	35 ÷ 5 = 7
4 × 5 = 20	5 × 4 = 20	30 ÷ 5 = 6
5 × 5 = 25	5 × 5 = 25	25 ÷ 5 = 5
6 × 5 = 30	5 × 6 = 30	20 ÷ 5 = 4
7 × 5 = 35	5 × 7 = 35	15 ÷ 5 = 3
8 × 5 = 40	5 × 8 = 40	10 ÷ 5 = 2
9 × 5 = 45	5 × 9 = 45	5 ÷ 5 = 1
10 × 5 = 50	5 × 10 = 50	0 ÷ 5 = 0

	×10	÷10
0 × 10 = 0	10 × 0 = 0	100 ÷ 10 = 10
1 × 10 = 10	10 × 1 = 10	90 ÷ 10 = 9
2 × 10 = 20	10 × 2 = 20	80 ÷ 10 = 8
3 × 10 = 30	10 × 3 = 30	70 ÷ 10 = 7
4 × 10 = 40	10 × 4 = 40	60 ÷ 10 = 6
5 × 10 = 50	10 × 5 = 50	50 ÷ 10 = 5
6 × 10 = 60	10 × 6 = 60	40 ÷ 10 = 4
7 × 10 = 70	10 × 7 = 70	30 ÷ 10 = 3
8 × 10 = 80	10 × 8 = 80	20 ÷ 10 = 2
9 × 10 = 90	10 × 9 = 90	10 ÷ 10 = 1
10 × 10 = 100	10 × 10 = 100	0 ÷ 10 = 0